AF407605

# THINK
## —— LIKE A ——
## *Women*

### "Decoding Mans Mind Through Her Eyes"

By Coco Paye

By Coco Paye

# Table of Contents

# Introduction

"Think Like a Woman : Decoding a Woman's Eyes" is a book that aims to provide insights and understanding into the male perspective by adopting a woman's point of view. It is intended to help women navigate and understand the complexities of men's thoughts, emotions, and behaviors in relationships. The book may offer tips, advice, and strategies for improving communication and building stronger connections with men.

Delving deep into the complexities of the male psyche, explores the underlying societal expectations and gender roles that shape men's thoughts and behaviors. By decoding these entrenched mindsets, readers can gain invaluable insights into their own decision-making processes and understand how these impact their relationships with women. While many books have focused on teaching women how to understand men, "Decoding the Male Mind" takes a refreshing approach by presenting a woman's perspective. By offering this new viewpoint, I bring a fresh and valuable understanding of the male psyche to the table.

Inspired by Steve Harvey's book, "Think Like A Man," "Decoding the Male Mind" adds a new dimension to the conversation. It challenges conventional beliefs and provides a thought-provoking exploration of the intricacies behind male behavior and thinking patterns. By gaining insights into the male mind through this woman's perspective, readers can enhance their understanding of men and improve their relationships.

# Chapter 1: Understanding Gender Differences

## The Power of Perspective

In the journey of understanding the complexities of human relationships, one aspect that often goes unnoticed is the power of perspective. As men, we often are trying to decipher the inner workings of a woman's mind, struggling to comprehend her thoughts and emotions. But what if we told you that the key to decoding the mysteries of a woman's mind lies in understanding her perspective? Welcome to "Thinking Like a Woman," a book that aims to bridge the gap between the genders and unravel the secrets of the female psyche.

"The Power of Perspective," we delve into the fundamental idea that thinking like a woman is not just about understanding her actions, but rather embracing her unique viewpoint on life. By immersing ourselves in the female perspective, we gain invaluable insights into her hopes, fears, desires, and dreams. Understanding a woman's perspective isn't about assuming a superior position or trying to manipulate emotions. It is about acknowledging and respecting the differences that exist between genders.

By doing so, we foster an environment of empathy, compassion, and mutual understanding. The Power of Perspective. In the journey of understanding the complexities of human relationships, one aspect that often goes unnoticed is the power of perspective. As men, we often are trying to decipher the inner workings of a woman's mind, struggling to comprehend her thoughts and emotions. Promoting understanding and empathy.

Thinking from a woman's perspective helps break down traditional gender stereotypes and biases. It allows men to challenge their own preconceived notions about women and recognize that gender does not determine abilities, interests, or worth. Building healthy relationships, men make an effort to understand a woman's perspective, it demonstrates respect for her autonomy, thoughts, and feelings. This fosters healthier and more equal relationships based on trust, open communication, and mutual support. Addressing gender inequality:

Enhancing problem-solving: Collaborating with women and considering their perspectives can bring diverse ideas, insights, and solutions to the table. This diversity of thought can lead to more innovative problem-solving and decision-making. Encouraging inclusivity in society: Considering a woman's perspective encourages inclusivity in various aspects of life, such as workplace policies, social norms, and cultural practices.

It helps create a society that values and respects the unique experiences and contributions of all genders. Remember, this does not mean that men should try to speak for or explain women's experiences. Instead, it involves actively listening to and learning from women, recognizing their knowledge and expertise, and supporting their right to autonomy and equality.

Understanding a woman's perspective can help foster better communication, empathy, and inclusivity in all areas of life. As I aims to shed light on some of the unique experiences and challenges that women often face, providing a broad understanding of their perspective. One important aspect to consider is the societal expectations placed on women. Throughout history, women have been assigned traditional roles, such as being homemakers and caregivers. While these roles are valuable, they can also limit opportunities for women to pursue their own aspirations and career goals.

In order to have a comprehensive understanding of the woman's perspective, it is important to consider how these factors interact and contribute to different experiences and challenges. Its important to understanding a woman's perspective entails recognizing and supporting women's choices and aspirations, addressing gender inequalities, challenging beauty standards. In the journey of understanding the complexities of human relationships, one aspect that often goes unnoticed is the power of perspective.

What if, I told you that the key to decoding the mysteries of a woman's mind lies in understanding her perspective? Through the lens of a woman, we can decode the intricacies of a man's mind. By examining the world from her eyes, we gain a fresh perspective on our own thoughts and actions. This newfound awareness allows us to communicate more effectively, build stronger relationships, and create a harmonious space where both genders can thrive.

These principles provide a framework for navigating relationships with intentionality and care. By adopting them, individuals can foster an environment conducive to love and emotional well-being. The cultivation of trust allows for a strong sense of security and openness, while effective communication enables the exchange of ideas, feelings, and needs in a clear and respectful manner. Moreover, these principles encourage personal growth, as individuals support each other's development and engage in continuous learning alongside their partner

## Think Like A Woman Explained

"Think Like A Woman", In this chapter, we explore various aspects of a woman's perspective. I am encouraging men to adapt to a mindset that aligns with how women typically think and perceive the world. It also means attempting to understand and empathize with the unique experiences, perspectives, and challenges that women face, in order to develop a deeper understanding and awareness of gender-related issues. By thinking like a woman, men can gain insight into the diverse perspectives and contribute to better communication

So, whether you are a man seeking to understand the woman in your life or simply someone curious about the female perspective, "Through Her Lens: Mastering the Art of Thinking Like a Woman" is your guidebook. Join us on this transformative journey as we unlock the power of perspective, decode the mysteries of the female mind, and cultivate deeper, more meaningful relationship

No one has the "keys" to forcing someone else to change or adapt to their partner's perspective. Building a healthy and fulfilling relationship isn't about having a magic wand, but rather about learning, understanding, and having compassion for one another. Women make up half of the global population. By thinking like a woman, men can better understand us and this becomes a win-win! In essence, thinking like a woman allows men to foster better relationships and more harmonious partnership, leading to a win-win situation for all involved.

## Unveiling the Gender Stereotypes

In our society, gender stereotypes have played big part, in the way men and women perceive themselves and each other. These deeply ingrained preconceived notions often hinder our ability to truly understand one another. In this subchapter, we aim to shed light on the gender stereotypes that have shaped our thinking and provide a fresh perspective on bridging the gap between the sexes.

Men, anybody, listen up – it's time to challenge the status quo and embrace a new way of thinking. In "Through Her Lens: Mastering the Art of Thinking Like a Woman," we delve into the intricacies of decoding the male mind through the eyes of a woman. By understanding gender stereotypes, we can dismantle the barriers that prevent meaningful connections from forming.

Firstly, let's acknowledge that gender stereotypes are not exclusive to women. Men have also been subjected to societal expectations that dictate how they should behave, think, and express themselves. By examining these stereotypes, we can begin to unravel the complexities of the male psyche and uncover the true essence of masculinity.

Stereotypes often portray women as emotional and irrational beings, while men are seen as logical and decisive. However, these stereotypes fail to recognize the multidimensionality of human nature. Men, it's crucial to understand that women are just as capable of logical thinking as you are. By embracing the art of thinking like a woman, you can tap into a wealth of emotional intelligence and gain a deeper understanding of yourself and those around you.

Furthermore, gender stereotypes have perpetuated the notion that women are solely responsible for nurturing and caregiving, while men are expected to be the providers and protectors. However, these roles aren't essential to challenge these stereotypes in order to foster equality and mutual understanding. By breaking free from these constraints, both men and women can embrace their true selves and live more fulfilling lives.

In « Unveiling the Gender Stereotypes" preconceived notions that have hindered our ability to truly understand one another. By challenging gender stereotypes, we can bridge the gap between the sexes and create a society that promotes equality and mutual respect. Men, anybody, it's time to think like a woman and decode the male mind through her eyes. Let us embark on this journey together, unraveling the complexities of gender stereotypes and embracing a new way of thinking such as.

Gender Roles: Traditional gender roles often assign specific responsibilities to women, such as household chores and child-rearing, while expecting men to be the primary providers and display assertiveness. These roles can restrict individual freedoms and hinder the development of equal partnerships. Emotional Expression: Society tends to stereotype women as more emotional and nurturing, while men are expected to be stoic and less emotional. These assumptions can limit emotional expression and communication within relationships, preventing a deeper understanding and connection between partners. Decision-Making: There may be assumptions that men should make important decisions or hold more power in the relationship. This can undermine a woman's autonomy and limit her ability to participate equally in decision-making processes.

It Is important to recognize and challenge these assumptions and stereotypes in order to foster healthier and more egalitarian relationships. By promoting open communication, shared responsibilities, and mutual respect, individuals can work towards building partnerships based on equality and understanding.

# Chapter 2: Embracing Empathy

## The Role of Empathy in Relationships

In the intricate dance of relationships, empathy plays a vital role that cannot be underestimated. It is a powerful tool that allows one to truly understand and connect with another person on a deeper level. In this subchapter, we will explore the significance of empathy in relationships, particularly from the unique perspective of thinking like a woman and decoding a man's mind through her eyes.

Empathy, often associated with the feminine approach to emotions, is not limited to any gender. Men, anybody, can bene t tremendously from cultivating empathy in their relationships. By developing this skill, men can gain a profound understanding of their partner's thoughts, feelings, and needs, leading to more harmonious and fulfilling connections.

One of the fundamental aspects of empathy is the ability to listen actively. When a man listens attentively to his partner, he demonstrates that he values her thoughts and opinions. This creates a safe space for her to express herself openly, fostering trust and emotional intimacy. By truly hearing and understanding her perspective, a man can bridge the gap between their different ways of thinking, thereby strengthening their bond.

Empathy also empowers men to provide emotional support to their partners. Understanding a woman's emotions goes beyond simply acknowledging them; it involves validating her experiences and offering comfort when she needs it most. By being empathetic, a man can offer a genuine shoulder to lean on, showing his partner that he truly cares about her well-being.

Furthermore, empathy plays a crucial role in conflict resolution. When disagreements arise, men who think like a woman can approach these situations with empathy, seeking to understand their partner's viewpoint instead of solely defending their own. This empathetic approach allows for open communication, compromise, and ultimately, resolution.

In the realm of romance, empathy allows men to anticipate in their partner's needs and desires. By putting themselves in her shoes, men can better understand and cater to her emotional and physical needs, enhancing the overall satisfaction and happiness in the relationship. Empathy is crucial in relationships as it strengthens emotional connections, enhances communication, resolves conflicts, builds trust, meets emotional needs, and fosters emotional intimacy. Cultivating empathy involves active listening, understanding, and validating the emotions of our loved ones, and responding with compassion and support. By practicing empathy, we create a nurturing and supportive environment in our relationships.

Overall empathy serves as a powerful tool that men, anybody, can use to strengthen their relationships. By thinking like a woman and decoding a man's mind through her eyes, men can gain a deeper understanding of their partner's emotions, needs, and desires. Through active listening, emotional support, conflict resolution, and fulfilling their partner's needs, empathy becomes a cornerstone of a successful relationship. So, open your heart, embrace empathy, and watch your relationships grow like never before.

## Nurturing Emotional Intelligence

In today's fast-paced world, emotional intelligence has become a crucial skill for success in both personal and professional relationships. Understanding and effectively managing emotions can lead to better communication, stronger connections, and a greater sense of empathy towards others.

For men, developing emotional intelligence can be particularly important in bridging the gap between genders and creating harmonious relationships. In the subchapter "Nurturing Emotional Intelligence" of the book "Think Like A Woman, Decoding Man's Mind Through Her Eyes", we delve into the secrets of decoding a man's mind through the eyes of a woman. I'm helping men understand the importance of emotional intelligence and providing practical tips for its cultivation.

Emotional intelligence is the ability to recognize, understand, and manage emotions in oneself and others. It involves being aware of one's own emotions and how they impact behavior, as well as being able to empathize with others and respond appropriately to their emotions. By nurturing emotional intelligence, men can gain a deeper understanding of themselves and improve their relationships with women. To develop emotional intelligence, self-awareness is key.

Men must learn to recognize and understand their own emotions, as well as the underlying reasons behind them. This self-reflection allows for better self-regulation, empowering men to manage their emotions in a healthy and constructive manner. Additionally, nurturing emotional intelligence involves enhancing empathy towards women. By putting themselves in a woman's shoes, men can gain a new perspective on their thoughts, feelings, and experiences.

This understanding fosters open and honest communication, leading to better relationships. "Nurturing Emotional Intelligence" provides practical exercises and strategies for men to enhance their emotional intelligence. Through various techniques, such as journaling, mindfulness, and active listening, men can develop a deeper understanding of emotions and learn to respond to them effectively.

By mastering emotional intelligence, men you'll definitely bridge the gap between genders and develop stronger connections with women. Whether you are a man seeking to understand women better or anybody interested in developing emotional intelligence, "Thinking Like a Woman". Discover the power of emotional intelligence and unlock the secrets of the female mind, ultimately leading to more meaningful and harmonious relationships.

## Developing a Deeper Understanding

In the journey of mastering the art of thinking like a woman, developing a deeper understanding of the opposite sex is crucial. In this subchapter, we will delve into the intricacies of decoding a man's mind through a woman's eyes. Whether you are a man seeking to comprehend the female perspective or anyone interested in bridging the gender gap, this section aims to provide valuable insights and practical advice.

Understanding the complexities of the male psyche requires empathy, patience, and an open mind. Men, anybody, can greatly bene t from adopting a woman's perspective, as it allows for a more balanced and harmonious approach to relationships and communication. By stepping into her shoes, you will gain a fresh understanding of the challenges women face daily, empowering you to build stronger connections and fostering mutual respect.

Decoding a man's mind begins with acknowledging that men and women have different ways of thinking, processing emotions, and expressing themselves. It is essential to recognize that these differences are not intended to create divisions but rather to enhance the richness and diversity of human interactions.

One crucial aspect of understanding men is recognizing woman's need for independence and self-sufficient. Men often value their autonomy and may have different ways of coping with stress and emotions. By acknowledging and respecting these differences, women can create a safe space where men feel comfortable expressing their thoughts and feelings without judgment or criticism.

Another key step in developing a deeper understanding is active listening. Men, anybody, can benefit from listening skills. When you truly allow yourself to truly hear and comprehend what women are expressing. By listening attentively, you can gain insights into their experiences, desires, and needs. Trust me, this will lead to better connections with your partner, based on shared understanding.

Listen to me please, when your partner feels acknowledged and validated is crucial in any relationship. When individuals feel valued and appreciated by their partner, it creates a strong sense of connection and fosters a deeper commitment. When both partners make an effort to ensure each other's happiness, it strengthens the bond between them. Not only does this contribute to overall mental health, but it also enhances the quality of the relationship as a whole.

Additionally, embracing vulnerability is crucial for both men and women. Encouraging and supporting men to express their vulnerability allows for a more authentic connection and paves the way for emotional growth. By understanding and accepting this vulnerability, women can create an environment that nurtures emotional intimacy, trust, and empathy.

In developing a deeper understanding of the opposite sex is a vital step in mastering the art of thinking like a woman.

By recognizing and appreciating the differences in how men think and express themselves, we can bridge the gender gap and foster meaningful connections. Men, anybody, can benefit from adopting a woman's perspective, enabling them to navigate relationships and communication with greater empathy and sensitivity. Through active listening, respecting autonomy, and embracing vulnerability, we can decode a man's mind through a woman's eyes, enhancing our understanding and appreciation for one another.

# Chapter 3: Communication Dynamics

## The Art of Active Listening

In the realm of understanding the complexities of human interaction, one skill stands out above all others - the art of active listening. In the pursuit of mastering the art of thinking like a woman, it is imperative for men, and anybody, to develop this vital skill. By decoding a man's mind through her eyes, one can truly tap into the essence of a woman's thoughts and emotions.

Active listening goes beyond simply hearing the words being spoken; it involves engaging with the speaker on a deeper level. It requires giving your undivided attention, both physically and mentally, to the person speaking. This means putting aside distractions, such as electronic devices, and truly focusing on the speaker's words and body language.

To actively listen, one must also be aware of their own biases and preconceived notions. By setting aside personal judgments and assumptions, it becomes easier to truly understand the other person's perspective. This is especially important when trying to think like a woman, as societal conditioning often leads to a disconnect between genders.

By actively listening, men can bridge this gap and gain insight into the female experience. It allows for a deeper understanding of her desires, fears, and motivations. Active listening also fosters empathy, as it enables men to truly put themselves in a woman's shoes and comprehend her unique perspective.

Practicing active listening involves several key techniques. Firstly, maintaining eye contact shows the speaker that their words are valued and respected. Additionally, nodding and using non-verbal cues, such as facial expressions, convey understanding and encouragement.

Active Listening: One of the most important aspects of effective communication is active listening. Women may have a need to express their emotions and concerns. By actively listening and showing empathy, you can make your partner feel heard and understood. Maintain eye contact, nod, and provide verbal cues to indicate your attentiveness.

I know women can be hard to understand. The key to a healthy relationship, Effective Communication Go hand in hand with, Active Listening. By giving your full attention to the person you're communicating with. These are the steps take notes. Maintain- eye contact, show genuine interest, and refrain from interrupting. This demonstrates respect and allows for a deeper understanding of their thoughts and feelings. Empathy and Understanding- Put yourself in the other person's shoes and try to understand their perspective.

Show empathy- by acknowledging and validating their emotions and experiences. Lastly- Be open-minded and willing to consider different viewpoints. Finally, asking open-ended questions encourages the speaker to delve deeper into their thoughts and feelings. This can lead to more meaningful and insightful conversations, providing valuable insights into the female psyche. Through the practice of active listening, we can truly master the art of thinking like a woman and unlock the secrets of the female mind.

## Non-Verbal Cues and Body Language

In the complex world of human communication, words are not the only means of expressing thoughts and emotions. Often, our non-verbal cues and body language speak louder than any words we could utter. They provide a glimpse into our true thoughts, desires, and feelings, allowing us to decode the mysteries of human interaction. In this subchapter, we will delve into the fascinating realm of non-verbal communication, exploring the subtle cues and body language that can help you understand the inner workings of a woman's mind.

As men, we sometimes struggle to understand the intricacies of a woman's thoughts and emotions. However, by learning to read and interpret non-verbal cues, we can gain valuable insights into her perspective. Understanding a woman's body language can help us decipher hidden messages, detect underlying emotions, and improve our overall communication skills.

One crucial aspect of non-verbal communication is facial expressions. The human face is a canvas of emotions, subtly revealing joy, sadness, surprise, or anger. Learning to recognize and interpret these expressions can give us a better understanding of what a woman is experiencing, even when her words may say otherwise.

Another crucial element is body posture and gestures. How a woman carries herself, the way she moves, and the positions she assumes can convey a wealth of information. For instance, crossed arms may indicate defensiveness or discomfort, while open and relaxed postures may suggest receptiveness and engagement.

Eye contact is yet another powerful non-verbal cue. The eyes can reveal a person's level of interest, trust, or truthfulness. By paying attention to a woman's eye movements, we can gauge her level of engagement and assess the authenticity of her words. Understanding non-verbal cues is not about becoming a mind reader; it is about becoming a more attentive and empathetic communicator. By sharpening our ability to read body language, we can bridge the gap between genders, fostering better understanding and connection.

In learning the differentiate between genuine and fake smiles, decipher the meaning behind different hand gestures, and unravel the mysteries behind subtle shifts in body posture. By mastering these skills, we can decode a man's mind through a woman's eyes, gaining a deeper understanding of her thoughts, desires, and emotions.

Men this is an enlightening journey into the world of non-verbal communication. Learn to think like a woman, and unlock the secrets hidden within her non-verbal cues and body language. By mastering these skills, you can become a more perceptive and effective communicator, fostering stronger connections and relationships with the women in your life.

## Effective Verbal Communication

In the intricate dance of relationships, communication holds the key to understanding and connection. Yet, for many men, deciphering the inner workings of a woman's mind can feel like an enigma wrapped in a mystery. It is in this realm that effective verbal communication becomes a vital tool, enabling men to bridge the gap and gain a deeper insight into the female perspective.

"Effective Verbal Communication," we delve into the art of understanding women by decoding their thoughts and emotions through her eyes. This section is a guide for men, anybody who seeks to bridge the communication gap and strengthen their relationships by thinking like a woman. Effective communication is important in any relationship. Men generally appreciate a partner who is open, understanding, and willing to listen. They want someone they can communicate with comfortably, resolving conflicts and discussing important matters openly.

To effectively communicate with women, it is crucial to listen attentively. Women often express themselves through subtle cues, nonverbal signals, and emotional undertones. By actively listening and paying attention to these nuances, men can gain a deeper understanding of a woman's perspective. It is through this process that the intricacies of her thoughts, desires, and needs will become clearer.

Furthermore, men must learn to communicate with empathy and understanding. Women often appreciate conversations that are rooted in emotional connection and genuine interest. By acknowledging her feelings and validating her experiences, men can create a safe and nurturing space for open dialogue. This empathetic approach allows women to feel understood and validated, leading to deeper connections and stronger bonds.

Additionally, it is vital for men to embrace vulnerability and express their own emotions. By sharing their thoughts and feelings, men can create an environment that encourages reciprocal sharing. This vulnerability fosters trust and allows women to feel comfortable expressing themselves openly. The result is a richer and more meaningful exchange of ideas and emotions.

Finally, mastering effective verbal communication requires practicing patience and avoiding assumptions. Men must be willing to ask questions and seek clarity when needed, rather than making assumptions based on their own perceptions. By fostering an open and non-judgmental environment, men can encourage women to share their thoughts and feelings freely.

In conclusion, effective verbal communication is an essential skill for men seeking to understand women. By actively listening, communicating with empathy and vulnerability, and practicing patience, men can decode the female perspective and strengthen their relationships. Through mastering the art of thinking like a woman, men can bridge the communication gap and foster deeper connections, leading to more fulfilling relationships.

# Chapter 4: Decoding Emotional Expression

## Embracing Vulnerability

In a society that often equates vulnerability with weakness, it can be challenging for anyone, regardless of gender, to fully embrace and understand its power. However, in the journey towards mastering the art of thinking like a woman, it becomes crucial for men, anybody, to decode the male mind through her eyes, and to recognize the significance of vulnerability in fostering deeper connections and personal growth.

The concept of vulnerability may seem foreign or uncomfortable to many men, as they are often conditioned to prioritize strength, independence, and self-reliance. However, when one opens up to vulnerability, they invite a unique opportunity for genuine connections and emotional intimacy, both with themselves and others. By embracing vulnerability, men can gain a deeper understanding of women's perspectives, experiences, and feelings.

When attempting to think like a woman, it is essential to recognize that vulnerability is not a sign of weakness, but rather an indication of strength and courage. It takes great courage to allow oneself to be seen and to express emotions openly, without fear of judgment or rejection. By embracing vulnerability, men can create an environment that encourages women to feel safe and understood, allowing for more meaningful and authentic relationships.

Moreover, vulnerability is a powerful tool for personal growth and self-discovery. By allowing oneself to be vulnerable, men can better navigate their own emotions, understand their desires, and identify areas of improvement. It is through vulnerability that one can truly explore their authentic self, breaking free from societal expectations and embracing their true passions and desires.

In the journey towards thinking like a woman, it is crucial to understand that vulnerability is a two-way street. Both men and women must be willing to embrace vulnerability, to create an equal and empathetic space for open communication and understanding. By recognizing vulnerability as a strength, men can bridge the gap between genders, fostering mutual respect, compassion, and empathy.

In conclusion, embracing vulnerability is a fundamental aspect of mastering the art of thinking like a woman. By understanding the power of vulnerability, men can decode the male mind through her eyes, fostering deeper connections, personal growth, and a more harmonious relationship between genders. Let us challenge societal norms, embrace vulnerability, and create a world where empathy and understanding thrive.

## Understanding Emotional Nuances

In the realm of human emotions, there exists a rich tapestry of nuances that can be both captivating and perplexing. For men, deciphering the emotional intricacies of women can often seem like a daunting task. However, by developing an understanding of these nuances, men can gain valuable insights into the female psyche and forge deeper connections with the women in their lives.

Emotional nuances are the subtle variations within different emotions that make them unique and complex. Each emotion is like a brushstroke on the canvas of the human experience, painting a vivid picture of our innermost thoughts and feelings. Women, in particular, possess a remarkable aptitude for navigating this emotional landscape, and by delving into their world, men can begin to decode the mysteries of their minds.

One of the key aspects of understanding emotional nuances is recognizing that emotions are not always straightforward. They can be layered, contradictory and multitude of factors such as past experiences, societal expectations, and personal values. By acknowledging and embracing this complexity, men can foster empathy and open up a space for authentic emotional expression.

Another crucial aspect of understanding emotional nuances is active listening. Women often communicate their emotions through subtle cues, both verbal and nonverbal. Paying attention to these cues can provide invaluable insights into their emotional state. It is important to remember that emotions are not always explicitly stated but can be conveyed through body language, tone of voice, or even through the silence between words.

Furthermore, understanding emotional nuances requires men to let go of preconceived notions and stereotypes. Each woman is unique, with her own set of experiences and perspectives. Avoid making assumptions based on societal expectations or generalizations. Instead, approach each woman with an open mind and a willingness to learn and understand her individual emotional landscape.

By grasping the significance of emotional nuances, men have the opportunity to forge deeper connections with the women in their lives. When men can appreciate and validate a woman's emotions, it creates a safe and nurturing environment for her to express herself fully. This, in turn, fosters trust, intimacy, and a deeper understanding between partners.

In understanding emotional nuances is a vital skill for men to develop when seeking to decode the complexities of the female mind. By recognizing the layered nature of emotions, actively listening, and avoiding stereotypes, men can navigate the emotional landscape with greater ease and sensitivity. Through this understanding, men can cultivate connection.

## Supporting Emotional Well-being

In our journey to understanding the complexities of the female mind, it is crucial to address the topic of emotional well-being. Emotions play a signi cant role in shaping a woman's perspective and behavior. By supporting and nurturing her emotional well-being, you can create a stronger bond and deeper understanding in any relationship. This subchapter aims to guide men, and anyone seeking to comprehend the female mind, in supporting emotional well-being effectively.

First and foremost, it is important to acknowledge the depth and intensity of a woman's emotions. Women tend to have a broader emotional range, experiencing both highs and lows more intensely. Rather than dismissing or belittling these emotions, learn to embrace and validate them. By doing so, you create a safe space for her to express herself authentically.

Active listening is a powerful tool in supporting emotional well-being. When a woman shares her thoughts and feelings, give her your undivided attention. Avoid interrupting or providing solutions right away. Instead, focus on understanding her perspective and empathizing with her emotions. By actively listening, you demonstrate your genuine interest in her well-being and validate her experiences.

Another crucial aspect of supporting emotional well-being is providing reassurance and comfort during challenging times. Women often seek emotional support when facing difficulties. Instead of trying to x the problem immediately, offer a shoulder to lean on and a listening ear. Sometimes, all she needs is someone to understand and empathize with her emotions, rather than providing immediate solutions.

Encourage open communication about emotions and feelings. Society has conditioned women to be more in tune with their emotions, but it is equally essential for men to express and discuss their emotions openly. By fostering an environment where both partners can freely communicate their emotions, you create a stronger emotional connection and mutual understanding.

Lastly, self-care plays a vital role in supporting emotional well-being. Encourage and actively participate in activities that promote mental, emotional, and physical well-being. By taking care of yourself, you set an example and inspire her to prioritize her own well-being. It goes beyond physical attraction or shared interests and involves a mutual understanding, respect, and support for each other's emotional well-being.

In supporting a woman's emotional well-being requires patience, understanding, and active participation. By embracing her emotions, actively listening, providing reassurance, encouraging open communication, and practicing self-care, you can create a nurturing environment that fosters emotional well-being for both partners. Remember, emotional well-being is a lifelong journey, and by working together, you can master the art of thinking like a woman and decoding the man's mind through her eyes.

# Chapter 5: Appreciating Differences

## Celebrating Individuality

In a world that often tries to mold us into the roles and expectations, it is crucial to celebrate and embrace individuality. Appreciating Differences: Each person brings their own unique set of experiences, perspectives, and qualities to a relationship. By appreciating and valuing these differences, we create an environment that fosters acceptance, understanding, and respect. Embracing our diverse traits and backgrounds can lead to richer conversations, new insights, and a deeper appreciation for one another.

Celebrating Individuality: Recognizing and celebrating each other's individuality is essential for nurturing a strong connection. This involves supporting each other's personal goals, interests, and growth journeys. By encouraging and nurturing the unique qualities and talents of our partners, we contribute to their overall well-being and happiness. Celebrating each other's achievements and successes helps create a positive and supportive atmosphere in the relationship.

Throughout history, women have fought tirelessly for their rights and freedoms, breaking free from the shackles of societal norms. Today, we are witnessing a shift in mindset, with women in their roles and taking charge of their lives. Understanding and celebrating individuality is a crucial step towards building stronger relationships, fostering empathy, and breaking down gender barriers.

By thinking like a woman and decoding the male mind through her lens. By celebrating individuality, men can gain valuable insights into the diverse experiences of women. This understanding can lead to more meaningful connections, better communication, and enhanced empathy. Celebrating individuality means acknowledging that every woman is unique, with her own dreams, aspirations, and perspectives.

It is about recognizing that no two women are the same, and each one brings something valuable to the table. By appreciating these differences, men can learn to navigate relationships with empathy and respect. I highlights the importance of open-mindedness and active listening when seeking to understand a woman's point of view. By embracing individuality, men can break away from stereotypes and preconceived notions, allowing them to truly see a woman for who she is – a multifaceted individual with her own thoughts, feelings, and desires. Through this lens, we can create a world where both men and women are free to express their true selves, breaking the barriers that restrict us and embracing the beauty of diversity.

## Respecting Personal Boundaries

In the complex world of relationships, understanding and respecting personal boundaries is crucial for maintaining healthy connections. Whether you are a man trying to navigate the intricate landscape of the female mind or anyone seeking to enhance their emotional intelligence, this subchapter, titled "Respecting Personal Boundaries," will provide invaluable insights to help you decode the male psyche through a woman's lens.

Personal boundaries are the emotional, physical, and mental limits we set to protect ourselves. They de ne what is acceptable and what is not, creating a sense of security and autonomy. Recognizing and honoring these boundaries is fundamental for fostering trust, mutual respect, and a harmonious connection with others. Autonomy and Individuality: Respecting personal boundaries acknowledges and respects each individual's autonomy and right to make decisions about their own body, time, and personal space.

It recognizes that everyone has their own limits, preferences, and comfort zones, and that these should be honored. When it comes to women, understanding their personal boundaries is important. Women have unique experiences, perspectives, and sensitivities that can differ greatly from those of men. By recognizing and respecting these boundaries, you will be able to forge deeper and more meaningful connections with the women in your life.

Firstly, it is essential to acknowledge that personal boundaries vary from person to person. What may be acceptable for one woman may be considered a breach of boundaries for another. Therefore, open communication and active listening are paramount. Take the time to engage in sincere conversations, ask questions, and genuinely listen to the responses. This will allow you to gain a deeper understanding of each woman's individual boundaries.

Respecting personal boundaries also means accepting and honoring the word "no." If a woman expresses discomfort or clearly states her boundaries, it is crucial to respect her wishes. Pushing past these boundaries not only erodes trust but can also cause emotional harm. Remember that consent and respect go hand in hand. Finally, it is vital to recognize that personal boundaries can change over time. As individuals grow and evolve, their boundaries may shift and transform.

Regularly checking in with your female counterparts and staying attuned to their changing needs will help you nurture a healthy and respectful relationship. Understanding and respecting personal boundaries is an indispensable skill for anyone seeking to connect on a deeper level with women. By embracing the insights shared in this subchapter, you will master the art of thinking like a woman, decoding the male mind through her eyes, and fostering authentic and fulling relationships.

## Honoring Emotional Needs

In the journey of understanding the complexities of relationships, it is essential for men to recognize and honor the emotional needs of women. By delving into the realm of emotions, men can gain valuable insights into the female perspective and develop a deeper connection with their partners. In this subchapter, we will explore the significant of acknowledging and addressing emotional needs, empowering men to think like a woman and decode the male mind through her eyes.

## Understanding the Female Emotional Landscape:

Women possess a rich emotional landscape that shapes their experiences and interactions. It is crucial for men to cultivate empathy and awareness, recognizing that emotions play a central role in a woman's life. By acknowledging this fundamental aspect, men can bridge the gap between the male and female psyche, fostering a more harmonious and fulfilling relationship.

## Effective Communication:

Communication lies at the heart of any successful relationship. To truly think like a woman, men must develop their communication skills, focusing on active listening and open dialogue. By attentively listening to a woman's emotions, concerns, and desires, men can create an environment where emotional needs are valued and understood. This not only facilitates better understanding but also strengthens the bond between partners.

## Creating Emotional Safety:

Creating an environment of emotional safety is paramount for women to express themselves freely. Men must provide a nurturing and non-judgmental space where women feel comfortable sharing their emotions without fear of retribution or dismissal. By validating and respecting their emotional needs, men can foster trust and intimacy, resulting in a deeper connection.

# Emotional Intelligence:

Developing emotional intelligence is an essential aspect of thinking like a woman. By honing this skill, men can navigate the complex emotional terrain, recognizing and responding to the needs of their partners. Emotional intelligence empowers men to be more attuned to their own emotions as well, creating a strong foundation for authentic and meaningful relationships.

Lastly: Honoring the emotional needs of women is a transformative journey that allows men to think like a woman and decode the male mind through her eyes. By understanding the female emotional landscape, enhancing communication, creating emotional safety, and developing emotional intelligence, men can forge stronger connections and build lasting relationships.

 Recognizing and respecting emotional needs is the key to unlocking a deeper level of understanding, empathy, and love between partners. So, let us embark on this enlightening journey together, and master the art of thinking like a woman.

# Chapter 6: Building Healthy Relationships

## Establishing Trust and Respect

In the intricate dance of human relationships, trust and respect form the foundation upon which connections are built. These two pillars are particularly crucial when it comes to understanding and connecting with women. To truly think like a woman and decode a man's mind through her eyes, it is imperative to establish trust and respect.

Trust is the bedrock of any successful relationship, be it with a partner, friend, or colleague. For men seeking to understand the female perspective, trust is the key that unlocks the door to her inner world. Creating an environment of trust requires consistent honesty, reliability, and open communication. Women appreciate men who keep their word, show up when needed, and share their thoughts and feelings authentically. Being a man of integrity is not only attractive but also paves the way for an honest exchange of emotions and experiences.

Respect, on the other hand, is the bridge that connects different perspectives and allows for mutual understanding. To truly think like a woman, it is essential to respect her unique experiences, emotions, and opinions. Recognize that her thoughts and feelings are just as valid as your own, even if they differ. Respecting her boundaries, both physical and emotional, is paramount. Treat her as an equal, valuing her contributions and nurturing her ambitions. By showing respect, you create an environment where she feels safe to express herself fully, leading to a deeper connection and understanding.

Building trust and respect cannot happen overnight; it requires time, effort, and patience. It is a continual process of learning and growing together. Practice active listening, empathize with her experiences, and seek to understand rather than judge. Be open to feedback and willing to adjust your behavior when necessary. Remember, trust and respect are not given automatically; they are earned through consistent actions and genuine care.

By establishing trust and respect, you will not only gain insight into the female perspective but also foster a more meaningful relationship with women in general. Through these foundational elements, you can bridge the gap between genders and truly think like a woman, unraveling the mysteries of a man's mind through her lens. Establishing Trust and Respect

In cultivating trust and respect is essential for anyone seeking to understand and connect with women. By embodying these qualities, men can unlock the door to a woman's inner world and gain invaluable insights into their thoughts and emotions. Trust and respect provide the foundation for open communication, mutual understanding,.. So, embark on this journey of thinking like a woman, decoding a man's mind through her eyes, and watch as your connections with women deepen and flourish.

## Effective Conflict Resolution

Conflict is an inevitable part of any relationship, whether it be personal or professional. In order to maintain healthy and harmonious connections, it is crucial to develop effective conflict resolution skills.. Understanding the different perspectives and communication styles between men and women can greatly contribute to successful resolution. Men, anybody who wishes to enhance their conflict resolution abilities, will find this chapter particularly beneficial.

By learning to think like a woman, individuals can gain a deeper understanding of their own emotion. One key aspect of effective conflict resolution is active listening.

Women are known for their ability to empathize and listen attentively, which allows them to grasp the underlying emotions and concerns behind a conflict. By adopting this valuable skill, men can create a safe and supportive environment where both parties can express their feelings openly, leading to a more comprehensive understanding .

Learn from the Conflict: Conflict can be an opportunity for personal growth and learning. Reflect on the conflict and identify any patterns or triggers that may have contributed. Consider how you can handle similar situations differently in the future to prevent recurring conflicts. Express Yourself Clearly: Use "I" statements to express your thoughts and feelings without blaming or attacking the other person. This helps to avoid defensiveness and encourages open dialogue. Clearly state your concerns and needs while being respectful and considerate.

Remember, effective conflict resolution requires patience, empathy, and a willingness to find common ground. By approaching conflicts with respect and a desire for resolution, you can foster stronger relationships and build trust with others. Seek Compromise: Be open to finding a middle ground or a compromise that works for both parties. This may require flexibility and a willingness to let go of rigid positions. Collaboratively brainstorm solutions and be willing to make concessions for the sake of resolving the conflict.

By thinking like a woman and decoding a man's mind through her eyes. By adopting key principles Through Her Lens: Mastering the Art of Thinking Like a Woman, you gain upper. Try to empathize with the other person's point of view and consider their feelings and needs. This understanding can help find common ground and reach a resolution

## Nurturing Intimacy and Connection

Intimacy and connection are the cornerstones of any successful relationship. However, understanding how to nurture and cultivate these aspects can often feel like a mystery to many men. In this subchapter, we will delve into the secrets of nurturing intimacy and connection by thinking like a woman and decoding the man's mind through her eyes.

To truly connect with a woman, it is crucial to understand her emotional needs and desires. Women thrive on emotional connection, and by tapping into this aspect, men can cultivate a deep level of intimacy. One way to do this is by actively listening and empathizing with her. By truly hearing her words, understanding her emotions, and offering support, men can create a safe space for vulnerability and emotions.

Another key aspect of nurturing intimacy is by fostering open and honest communication. Women appreciate men who are willing to have meaningful conversations about their thoughts, fears, and aspirations. By creating an environment where both partners feel comfortable expressing their innermost thoughts, a stronger connection can be built. This requires men to be receptive and non-judgmental, allowing women to feel heard and understood.

In addition to emotional connection, physical touch is also crucial in nurturing intimacy. Women often comfort and security in physical affection, whether it be holding hands, cuddling, or simply hugging. These small gestures can go a long way in conveying love and care, strengthening the bond between partners.

Intimacy for women is just as important as it is for men in a relationship. Intimacy can encompass emotional, physical, and sexual aspects, and it is important for both partners to feel connected and fulfilled in these areas. It is essential to create a safe and supportive environment where a woman feels comfortable expressing her desires, needs, and boundaries related to intimacy. This involves open communication, mutual respect, and a willingness to listen and understand each other a deeper level of emotional closeness and satisfaction in the relationship.

Furthermore, nurturing intimacy and connection requires investing time and effort into the relationship. Making an active effort to create shared experiences, such as going on dates, planning surprise outings, or engaging in activities together, can help in fostering a deeper connection. By continuously showing interest and investing in the relationship, men can demonstrate their commitment and dedication.

In conclusion, nurturing intimacy and connection is essential for any successful relationship. By thinking like a woman and decoding the man's mind through her eyes, men can gain insights into the emotional needs and desires of their partners. By actively listening, fostering open communication, engaging in physical touch, and investing time and effort, men can create a strong foundation of intimacy and connection.

## Intimacy For Women

When comes to intimacy, It's essential to remember that every woman is unique and has her preferences and desires. However, there are some general aspects that many women often appreciate in intimate relationships. Here are a few things that many women tend to enjoy when it comes to intimacy;

Emotional Connection: Woman are often prioritize emotional intimacy and connection in their relationships. Building trust, open communication, and being attentive to her emotional needs can deepen the bond and create a more fulfilling intimate experience.

Respect/Consent: **Respecting boundaries** is crucial in any relationship. Women appreciate partners who value their autonomy, listen to their needs, and seek their consent at every stage of intimacy. It's important to prioritize open and honest conversations about comfort levels and desires.

Foreplay/Seduction: Many women enjoy a combination of physical and emotional stimulation before engaging in sexual activity. Taking the time for foreplay and seduction allows for increased arousal and can enhance overall satisfaction.

Communication/Active-Listening: Discussing desires, fantasies, and preferences openly is important to understand what pleases her. Women appreciate partners who actively listen, show a genuine interest in their pleasure, and adapt accordingly.

Slow and Sensual Approaches: Some women prefer a more gradual, sensual approach to intimacy rather than rushing into sexual activity. Taking the time to explore each other's bodies, engage in non-sexual touch, and create a relaxed and comfortable atmosphere can enhance the overall experience.

When comes to intimacy, It's essential to remember that every woman is unique and has her preferences and desires. However, there are some general aspects that many women often appreciate in intimate relationships. Here are a few things that many women tend to enjoy when it comes to intimacy;

It Is important for partners to actively engage in conversations about their expectations, boundaries, and desires regarding intimacy. This openness can help prevent misunderstandings and promote a deeper understanding of each other's needs and preferences.

Regularly checking in with each other and discussing what feels pleasurable, comfortable, and fulfilling can contribute to a healthier and more satisfying intimate relationship. Listening with empathy, being non-judgmental, and creating a safe space for these conversations can help foster a stronger connection and prevent conflicts from arising.

Additionally, regular communication helps partners grow together and adapt to any changes in desires or needs over time. Being receptive to each other's feedback and understanding that intimacy is a dynamic aspect of a relationship can contribute to a more fulfilling and harmonious partnership.

This is the ultimate goal for anyone who has been in a relationship. The principles for a healthier and better relationship can be applicable to anyone currently in or seeking a relationship. These principles create a structure for navigating relationships with purpose and consideration. By embracing these principles, individuals can create an environment that nurtures love and emotional well-being.

# Chapter 7: Empowering Women

## Recognizing Women's Strengths

Recognizing Women's Strengths" from the book "Through Her Lens: Mastering the Art of Thinking Like a Woman," we delve into the unique qualities and strengths that women possess. Addressed to a diverse audience of men and anyone interested in understanding the female perspective, this subchapter aims to shed light on the intricacies of a woman's mind and help develop a deeper appreciation for women's strengths.

From time immemorial, women have been known for their emotional intelligence, empathy, and intuition. Their ability to understand and connect with others on a deeper level is unparalleled. Through this lens, men can gain valuable insights into their own relationships, both personal and professional, by recognizing and harnessing the power of these qualities.

Women's strengths lie in their ability to communicate effectively and establish meaningful connections. Their unique approach to problem-solving often involves collaboration, consensus building, and nurturing relationships. By embracing these strengths, men can cultivate healthier and more balanced dynamics in their interactions with women.

Decoding the male mind through a woman's eyes is a fascinating journey that allows for a deeper understanding of the complexities of human behavior. Women possess a keen sense of observation, enabling them to pick up on subtle cues, body language, and unspoken emotions. By learning to recognize and appreciate this skill, men can enhance their own communication and develop stronger connections with women.

Moreover, women's strengths extend beyond interpersonal relationships. They excel at multitasking, adaptability, and resilience. Balancing numerous responsibilities, women have become masters at managing their time and resources effectively. Men can learn from this strength, incorporating it into their own lives to achieve a greater sense of balance.

By recognizing and embracing women's strengths, men can foster an environment of equality and respect. It is crucial to acknowledge that these strengths are not exclusive to women but rather qualities that can be cultivated by anyone. Understanding and appreciating women's strengths will lead to more harmonious relationships, increased empathy, and a more inclusive society. "Recognizing Women's Strengths" is an essential subchapter in the book "Through Her Lens: Mastering the Art of Thinking Like a Woman."

It provides men and anyone interested in understanding women's perspectives with valuable insights into the unique qualities and strengths that women possess. By embracing and incorporating these strengths into their own lives, men can foster healthier relationships, enhance their communication skills, and contribute to a more inclusive society.

## Challenging Gender Bias

In our modern society, gender bias continues to persist, often unconsciously, shaping our thoughts, actions, and expectations. It limits individuals from reaching their full potential and hinders the progress of society as a whole. To overcome this, it is essential for men and anyone interested in promoting equality to challenge and dismantle these biases. In this subchapter, we will explore the importance of challenging gender bias and provide insights into thinking like a woman to decode a man's mind through her eyes.

Understanding gender bias requires introspection and an open mind. By examining our own beliefs and behaviors, we can identify the biases that have been ingrained in us from an early age. These biases may manifest in subtle ways, such as assuming traditional gender roles or underestimating women's abilities. By recognizing these biases, we can actively work to counter them and create a more inclusive society.

Thinking like a woman can be a powerful tool in challenging gender bias. By putting ourselves in a woman's shoes, we gain empathy and perspective on the unique struggles and experiences they face. This empathy allows us to challenge stereotypes and preconceived notions, promoting a more equal and understanding society.

Decoding a man's mind through a woman's lens is not about generalizing or making assumptions about all men. Instead, it is about recognizing the societal pressures and expectations placed on men, which can also perpetuate gender bias. By understanding these pressures, we can empathize with men's experiences and work towards breaking down harmful stereotypes.

To challenge gender bias effectively, we must engage in open and honest conversations. By listening to women's experiences and perspectives, we can gain valuable insights and learn from their wisdom. It is important to create safe spaces where women feel comfortable sharing their thoughts and ideas, free from judgment or dismissal. In turn, men can contribute to these conversations by sharing their own experiences and actively supporting gender equality.

Challenging gender bias is a crucial step towards creating a more inclusive and equal society. By thinking like a woman and decoding a man's mind through her eyes, we can gain empathy, challenge stereotypes, and actively work towards dismantling harmful biases. Together, men and anyone interested in promoting equality can create a world where everyone can thrive regardless of gender.

## Promoting Equality and Inclusion

In the subchapter "Promoting Equality and Inclusion" of the book "Through Her Lens: Mastering the Art of Thinking Like a Woman," we delve into the crucial topic of gender equality and the significance of fostering an inclusive society. This chapter is addressed to men, but its message is pertinent for anybody who seeks a deeper understanding of the female perspective and aims to contribute positively to gender dynamics.

Understanding the complexity of gender dynamics is key to promoting equality. It requires recognizing that women have historically faced systemic barriers and discrimination, which continue to shape their experiences today. By acknowledging these challenges, men can begin to empathize and actively work towards dismantling these barriers.

Promoting equality starts with self-reflection and a willingness to learn. By developing an awareness of their own biases and assumptions, men can challenge and unlearn societal norms that perpetuate inequality. Recognizing that gender equality bene ts everyone, men become allies in creating a more inclusive world.

Hey there, Picture this: when we make sure that women have a seat at the table, we unleash a powerhouse of diverse perspectives that can do extraordinary things. *Bam!* Their innovative ideas and fresh outlooks create a supercharged storm of well-rounded solutions. We're all about amplifying those incredible women's voices, giving them the recognition they've worked oh-so-hard for. Oh yeah! So, step aside, folks, because it's time to join the celebration and acknowledge their mind-blowing accomplishments. Get ready for an electrifying ride and let's rock the world together, as powerhouse couple!

Promoting equality and inclusion is not about diminishing men's experiences or diminishing the unique qualities they bring to the table. Rather, it is about recognizing that gender equality bene ts society as a whole. When women are empowered and treated as equals, it leads to greater innovation, improved decision-making, and a more harmonious and just society.

I aim to equip men, and anyone who wishes to understand the female perspective, with the tools necessary to promote equality and inclusion. By encouraging men to think like a woman, we can decode the male mind through her eyes, fostering empathy and understanding. Together, we can create a world where gender is not a barrier to success, where diversity is celebrated, and where equality and inclusion are the norm.

Let us embark on this transformative journey together, challenging our own biases, and advocating for equality and inclusion. By doing so, we pave the way for a brighter and more equitable future for all.

# Chapter 8: Cultivating Self-Awareness

## Reflecting on Personal Biases

In our journey to mastering the art of thinking like a woman, it is important to take a moment and reflect on our personal biases. As men, and indeed as human beings, we'll have our own set of biases that shape our perceptions and decisions. However, it is crucial to recognize that these biases can sometimes hinder our understanding of others, particularly when it comes to decoding a woman's mind through her eyes.

When it comes to gender dynamics, societal norms, and expectations, biases can run deep. These biases can be ingrained in us from a young age, perpetuated by media, culture, and even our own personal experiences. They can lead us to make assumptions or judgments about women that may not be accurate or fair. By re ecting on our biases, we can begin to challenge and reshape our thinking, allowing us to develop a more empathetic and understanding mindset.

One of the those steps in reflection on our personal biases is to acknowledge that they exist. It is natural to have preconceived notions about certain things, but it is crucial to be aware of them and their potential impact on our interactions with women. By acknowledging our biases, we can start to question them and actively seek alternative perspectives.

Another important aspect of reflecting on our biases is to listen and learn from women's experiences. Engaging in open and honest conversations with women, reading literature written by women, and seeking out diverse viewpoints can provide valuable insights into the lived experiences of women. It is essential to approach these conversations with an open mind and a willingness to challenge our own beliefs.

Furthermore, our personal biases requires us to examine the language we use, both in our thoughts and in our interactions. Language can be powerful and can inadvertently reinforce stereotypes or biases. By being mindful of the words we choose, we can create a more inclusive and respectful environment for everyone.

Reflecting on personal biases is a continuous journey that requires self-awareness and a commitment to growth.

Through this process, we can begin to dismantle the barriers that hinder our understanding of women's perspectives. By challenging our biases and actively seeking to think like a woman, we can develop a deeper sense of empathy, enhance our relationships, and create a more equitable society for all.

## Exploring Personal Growth

In the quest for self-improvement and understanding, it is essential to explore personal growth. This subchapter of "Think Like a Woman: Decoding Man's Mind Through Her Eyes" is dedicated to helping men understand the importance of personal growth and how it can be achieved by decoding the mind of a woman through her eyes.

Personal growth is a lifelong journey that allows individuals to become the best version of themselves. It involves constantly learning, evolving, and challenging oneself to break free from limiting beliefs and embrace new perspectives. While personal growth is often associated with women, men too can greatly bene t from this transformative process.

By thinking like a woman and decoding the male mind through her eyes, men can gain valuable insights into their own emotions, behaviors, and relationships. This understanding provides the foundation for personal growth, enabling men to cultivate self-awareness, empathy, and emotional intelligence.

Through the lens of a woman, men can also learn the art of effective communication and understanding. Women often prioritize emotional connection and empathetic listening, which can enhance relationships and foster personal growth. By embracing these qualities, men can build stronger bonds and gain a deeper understanding of themselves and others.

Furthermore, personal growth involves setting goals and pursuing them with determination and resilience. By thinking like a woman and decoding the male mind through her eyes, men can tap into their intuition and develop a clearer vision of what they want to achieve. With this newfound clarity, they can take purposeful actions and overcome obstacles on their path to personal growth.

By exploring personal growth is a vital component of for meaningful life. By thinking like a woman and decoding the male mind through her eyes, men can gain valuable insights that enable them to embark on a journey of self-improvement. Through self-reflection, effective communication, and goal setting, men can cultivate self-awareness, empathy, and resilience. Ultimately, personal growth allows individuals to break free from limiting beliefs, uncover their true potential, and create a life that aligns with their values and aspirations.

# Finding Authenticity and Fulfilment

In today's fast-paced world, both men and women are constantly seeking ways to find authenticity and fulfilment in their lives. However, , "Finding Authenticity and Fulfilment," will focus on a unique perspective - thinking like a woman and decoding a man's mind through her eyes. This chapter aims to provide valuable insights for men, anybody, who are eager to understand the female thought process and tap into their own authenticity and fulfillment.

Authenticity is the cornerstone of a fulfilling life. It enables individuals to embrace their true selves, make meaningful connections, and pursue their passions. For men, understanding the way women think can be a powerful tool in discovering their own authenticity. By learning to think like a woman, men can gain a deeper understanding of their own desires, emotions, and motivations.

Thinking like a woman doesn't mean adopting a feminine identity, but rather acknowledging and appreciating the unique perspectives and experiences that women bring to the table. By stepping into a woman's shoes, men can expand their worldview, challenge societal norms, and break free from the limitations imposed by rigid gender roles.

Decoding a man's mind through a woman's eyes involves empathy, active listening, and open-mindedness. By engaging in meaningful conversations with women and genuinely trying to understand their point of view, men can gain valuable insights into their own desires and needs. This process is not about conforming to societal expectations but about embracing one's true self.

"Finding Authenticity and Fulfillment," offers men, anybody, a unique perspective on self-discovery and personal growth. By thinking like a woman and decoding a man's mind through her eyes.. This journey requires an open mind, empathy, and a willingness to challenge societal norms. By embracing the qualities traditionally associated with femininity, men can unlock their true self.

"Finding Authenticity and Fulfillment" is a thought-provoking book that provides a unique perspective on self-discovery and personal growth, specifically targeting men but also applicable to anyone interested in understanding themselves better. The author takes on the perspective of a woman, offering insights into a man's mind through her eyes. This approach encourages readers to step outside of their usual viewpoint and consider alternative perspectives, leading to a deeper understanding of oneself and others.

# Chapter 9: The Art of Thinking Like a Woman

## Embracing Feminine Perspectives: Unlocking the Power of Understanding

Embracing Feminine Perspectives," we delve into the crucial concept of thinking like a woman and understanding the male mind through her eyes. This section of the book, "Through Her Lens: Mastering the Art of Thinking Like a Woman," is aimed at men, but is valuable for anyone seeking to bridge the gender gap and foster better relationships and communication.

In today's society, embracing feminine perspectives has become more important than ever. It is not about conforming to stereotypes or playing into gender roles, but rather about recognizing the unique experiences and insights that women bring to the table. By understanding and appreciating these perspectives, men can gain valuable insights that can enhance their personal and professional lives.

The art of thinking like a woman is not about mimicking or replicating their thought processes, but rather about developing empathy and compassion. It involves embracing a mindset that values emotional intelligence, intuition, and the importance of relationships. By doing so, men can tap into a wealth of knowledge that can help them navigate complex situations and make informed decisions.

Through this subchapter, we explore various aspects of the feminine perspective, providing practical guidance and thought-provoking insights. We delve into understanding women's needs, desires, and aspirations, which are often shaped by societal expectations and cultural norms. By decoding the nuances of a woman's mind, men can foster deeper connections, build trust, and create a more inclusive and harmonious environment.

Moreover, you'll unravels the power of effective communication and active listening. Men will learn how to truly understand and validate women's experiences, opinions, and emotions. By embracing feminine perspectives, men can overcome biases, challenge stereotypes, and foster a more equitable society.

"Embracing Feminine Perspectives" "Through Her Lens: Mastering the Art of Thinking Like a Woman," catering to anyone seeking to understand and appreciate the unique insights women possess. By embracing these perspectives, men can enhance their relationships, develop a deeper understanding of themselves, and contribute to a more balanced and inclusive world. So, let us embark on this enlightening journey of thinking like a woman and unlock the power of embracing feminine perspectives.

## Cultivating Empathy and Compassion Subchapter: Cultivating Empathy and Compassion

In a world where gender stereotypes have long dictated how men and women should think and behave, the notion of "thinking like a woman" may seem unconventional to some. However, the concept of empathizing and understanding others' emotions is not exclusive to any gender. In fact, cultivating empathy and compassion is a vital aspect of human connection and personal growth for anyone, regardless of their gender identity.

I wanted to delve into the significance of cultivating empathy and compassion and explore how adopting a more empathetic mindset. In doing so can can help decode a man's mind through a woman's eyes. By embracing these qualities, men can gain a deeper understanding of themselves, their relationships, and the world around them.

Empathy is the ability to understand and share the feelings of another person. It involves putting ourselves in someone else's shoes, actively listening, and validating their experiences. By practicing empathy, men can bridge the gap between genders, fostering healthier and more meaningful connections with the women in their lives.

Compassion, on the other hand, is the act of showing kindness, care, and understanding towards others, even in difficult circumstances. Cultivating compassion allows men to respond to the emotions and needs of women with patience and understanding. Men can gain a fresh perspective on the challenges women face in a patriarchal society. They can better comprehend the impact of societal expectations, gender biases, and the struggles that women often encounter in their personal and professional lives.

By mastering the art of cultivating empathy and compassion, men can embark on a transformative journey of self-discovery and personal growth. They can forge deeper connections with the women in their lives, gain insights into their own emotions and motivations, and ultimately contribute to building a more empathetic and compassionate world for all genders.

# Integrating Feminine and Masculine Qualities

In the pursuit of personal growth and understanding, it is essential to recognize and appreciate the unique qualities that both the feminine and masculine energies bring to our lives. Traditionally, society has boxed these energies into rigid stereotypes, limiting our ability to fully tap into their potential. However, by embracing and integrating both feminine and masculine qualities, we can unlock a new level of self-awareness and enrich our relationships with others.

The feminine energy embodies traits such as intuition, empathy, and nurturing. It encourages us to listen to our inner voice and connect with our emotions on a deeper level. By tapping into our feminine side, we can access a wellspring of creativity and intuition that can guide us in making more authentic and holistic decisions. This energy also allows us to cultivate deeper connections with others, as we become more attuned to their emotional needs and can offer support and understanding.

On the other hand, the masculine energy is associated with assertiveness, logic, and action. It urges us to be proactive, take risks, and pursue our goals with determination. By embracing our masculine qualities, we can tap into our problem-solving skills and analytical thinking, enabling us to make sound and rational decisions. This energy also encourages us to set boundaries, assert our needs, and take charge of our lives.

Integrating these seemingly distinct energies allows us to create a harmonious balance within ourselves. Men, in particular, can benefit immensely from embracing their feminine qualities. By cultivating empathy and emotional intelligence, they can develop stronger connections with their partners, friends, and family. It also allows them to access their creative potential, enabling them to think outside the box and come up with innovative solutions to problems.

This integration also helps women set boundaries, assert themselves, and stand up for their rights in a society that often undervalues their contributions. Ultimately, integrating feminine and masculine qualities is about embracing the full spectrum of human experience. It is about recognizing the strengths and limitations of both. So, let us embark on this journey of self discovery and explore the beauty that lies in integrating feminine and masculine qualities.

# Chapter 10: Applying New Perspectives

## Enhancing Relationships with Women

The art of enhancing relationships with women, offering valuable insights and strategies to help men better understand and connect with the women in their lives. Whether you're n a romantic relationship, a friendship, or simply seeking to improve your overall communication with women, this subchapter will provide you with the tools to navigate the complex and beautiful world of female thinking.

Understanding women can often feel like deciphering a secret code, but by adopting a thoughtful and empathetic approach, you can bridge the gap and build strong, meaningful connections. It is crucial to recognize that women perceive and process the world differently from men, and it is through their unique lens that we can truly understand their thoughts and emotions.

One key aspect of enhancing relationships with women is active listening. Women frequently communicate through subtle cues and non-verbal signals, so paying attention to these will not only help you understand them better but also make them feel valued and heard. By actively engaging in conversations and showing genuine interest, you can create a safe space for sharing thoughts, concerns, and aspirations.

Another vital element is empathy. Women often seek emotional connection and understanding, so putting yourself in their shoes will allow you to connect on a deeper level. Empathy involves recognizing and validating their emotions, rather than dismissing or trying to solve their problems. By offering support and understanding, you can foster trust and strengthen your bond.

Additionally, learning to appreciate and respect women's perspectives is crucial. Recognizing their unique strengths, experiences, and talents will not only boost their self-esteem but also enrich your relationships. Encourage their personal growth and celebrate their achievements, fostering an environment of mutual respect and admiration.

Furthermore, communication styles can impact relationships. Women often appreciate open, honest, and direct communication. Avoiding mind games and being transparent about your intentions will foster trust and create a solid foundation for a healthy connection.

Lastly, remember that every woman is unique, and there is no one-size- fits-all approach. By treating each woman as an individual with her own desires, needs, and aspirations, you can build authentic more successful relationships. Respect their boundaries, embrace their individuality, and appreciate the beauty of their perspectives.

By enhancing relationships with women requires a genuine desire to understand, connect, and appreciate their unique perspectives. By actively listening, empathizing, and respecting their individuality, you can forge deep and meaningful connections. Remember, it is through her lens that we can truly master the art of thinking like a woman and create lasting relationships based on mutual understanding and respect.

## Improving Communication with Women

Communication is the foundation of any successful relationship. Yet, for many men, understanding and effectively connecting with women can sometimes feel like deciphering a complex code. In this subchapter, we will explore valuable insights and practical strategies to help you improve your communication skills with women. Communication : allows us to truly listen and understand what the other person is saying. Instead of just waiting for our turn to speak, we actively engage in the conversation and try to grasp the emotions and thoughts behind the words. This creates a safe and open space for effective communication

Firstly, it is essential to recognize that women often have different communication styles and preferences compared to men. Understanding and appreciating these differences can pave the way for more meaningful interactions. Women tend to prioritize emotional connection, empathy, and active listening. They often value open and honest conversations that explore emotions and feelings. By being attentive, empathetic, and genuinely interested in what she has to say. This creates a safe and nurturing space for communication.

Next, it is crucial to be mindful of non-verbal communication cues. Women are often highly attuned to body language, facial expressions, and tone of voice. Paying attention to these subtle signals can provide valuable insights into her thoughts and feelings. Maintain eye contact, use open body language, and be mindful of your tone to ensure your non-verbal cues align with your words.

One effective strategy to improve communication with women is active listening. This means fully engaging in the conversation, rather than simply waiting for your turn to speak. Avoid interrupting or dismissing her thoughts and opinions. Instead, ask open-ended questions to encourage her to share more. Paraphrasing and summarizing her words can demonstrate that you are actively listening and seeking to understand her perspective.

Furthermore, it is important to be mindful of any biases or assumptions you may have about women's communication styles. Stereotypes can hinder effective communication and perpetuate misunderstandings. Approach each interaction with an open mind, allowing her to express herself without judgment.

Lastly, practice empathy and emotional intelligence. Women often appreciate partners who can understand and validate their emotions. Show your support by acknowledging her feelings and offering reassurance. Remember, empathy is not about fixing problems but rather showing understanding and compassion.

Improving communication with women is an ongoing process that requires patience, practice, and a genuine desire to connect. By incorporating these strategies into your interactions, you will lay the foundation for better communication, fostering stronger relationships with the women in your life. Remember, the key is to listen, understand, and respect her perspective, ultimately building a bridge of understanding between the genders.

## Thriving in a Gender-Equal World

Welcome to the subchapter "Thriving in a Gender-Equal World" from the insightful book, "Through Her Lens: Mastering the Art of Thinking Like a Woman." In this section, we address men and anybody who is eager to gain a deeper understanding of the female perspective and unlock the secrets of decoding a man's mind through a woman's eyes.

In today's society, the pursuit of gender equality has become an essential goal. It is crucial for men and women to work together as allies, empowering each other to create a more inclusive and harmonious world. This subchapter aims to shed light on the ways in which both genders can thrive in such an environment.

Firstly, understanding the challenges faced by women is paramount. By recognizing the systemic barriers that hinder their progress, men can actively contribute to dismantling these obstacles. It requires empathy, active listening, and a willingness to learn from the lived experiences of women. This subchapter will provide valuable insights into the struggles women face daily, helping men to develop a greater appreciation for the importance of gender equality.

Moreover, thriving in a gender-equal world necessitates embracing diversity and promoting inclusivity. By encouraging diverse perspectives and fostering an inclusive environment, men can create spaces that empower women to contribute fully and authentically. This subchapter will offer practical advice on how men can actively engage in creating a supportive and inclusive culture, bene ting both men and women alike.

Another crucial aspect of thriving in a gender-equal world is effective communication. Men often seek to understand women better, but the differences in communication styles can pose a challenge. Explore the nuances of female communication, helping men decipher the unspoken messages and decode the intricacies of a woman's mind. By mastering the art of effective communication, men can foster stronger relationships, enhance collaboration, and create a more harmonious environment.

Ultimately, thriving in a gender-equal world requires men to become true allies and advocates for gender equality. By supporting and uplifting women, men can contribute to a more balanced and equitable society.

## Women & Men Venus/ Mars Concept:

Men are from Mars, Women are from Venus" is a popular saying that originated from the title of a bestselling book by John Gray. The phrase suggests that men and women are fundamentally different in their thinking, communication styles, and emotional needs, to the extent that they might as well be from different planets.

"Men are from Mars" implies that men tend to be more logical, problem-solving oriented, and goal-oriented in their approach to relationships and communication. They may prioritize independence, self-sufficiency, and finding solutions rather than exploring emotions and discussing feelings openly.

"On the other hand, "Women are from Venus" suggests that women tend to be more emotional, empathetic, and relationship-focused. They may prioritize connection, communication, and expressing emotions in their approach to relationships. They may often seek understanding and empathy rather than immediately trying to solve problems.

While there may be similarities in the general idea of understanding and appreciating a woman's perspective, thinking like a woman from her eyes goes beyond the specific concepts outlined in the book "Men are from Mars, empathize with a woman's unique experiences, emotions, and perspectives in all aspects of life, not just relationships. It requires acknowledging and challenging societal norms and expectations.

## Mastering the Art of Thinking Like a Woman

"Through Her Lens: Mastering the Art of Thinking Like a Woman" has aimed to provide valuable insights into the female perspective, helping men and anyone interested in understanding the intricate workings of a woman's mind. By decoding the man's mind through her eyes, this book has offered a unique opportunity to bridge the communication gap and foster better relationships.

Throughout the chapters, we have explored various aspects of thinking like a woman, delving into the complexities of her emotions, desires, and thought processes. By gaining a deeper understanding of these elements, men can cultivate empathy, strengthen connections, and build healthier relationships with the women in their lives.

One of the key takeaways from this book is the importance of active listening. Women often communicate their thoughts and feelings indirectly, relying on subtle cues and nonverbal signals. By honing the skill of active listening, men can become attuned to these nuances, allowing for more effective communication and a greater understanding of what lies behind a woman's words.

Furthermore, understanding a woman's perspective involves recognizing the impact of societal and cultural factors on her experiences. By acknowledging the challenges and biases women face, men can support and empower them, contributing to a more inclusive and equitable society. .

Another crucial aspect highlighted in this book is the importance of respecting personal boundaries. By recognizing and honoring a woman's boundaries, men can create a safe and comfortable environment where she feels valued and heard. This fosters trust and allows for open and honest communication, enhancing the quality of relationships.

Ultimately, "Through Her Lens: Mastering the Art of Thinking Like a Woman" aims to encourage a shift in perspective, urging men and anyone interested in understanding women to embrace empathy, compassion, and open-mindedness. By adopting these qualities and actively seeking to understand the female experience, men can navigate relationships with greater sensitivity and forge deeper connections.

It Is my hope that this book serves as a guide, opening doors to a new way of thinking and facilitating meaningful connections between genders. By mastering the art of thinking like a woman, we can build a world where mutual understanding and respect thrive, fostering harmonious relationships and a more equitable society for all.

"Mastering the Art of Thinking Like a Woman" is all about embracing the unique perspectives and thought processes that women bring to the table. Here's a breakdown of how you can tap into this mindset:

1. Empathy and Emotional Intelligence: Women often have a natural ability to empathize and understand emotions, making them highly effective at connecting with others on a deeper level. Practice being aware of others' emotions and listening with empathy. This will help foster stronger relationships and create a more inclusive environment.

2. Collaboration and Communication: Women tend to excel in collaboration, valuing teamwork and collective decision-making. Foster an open and inclusive dialogue where all voices are heard and respected. Encourage active participation and create space for different ideas to flourish.

3. Problem-Solving and Flexibility: Women often approach problem-solving with a multidimensional mindset. They consider various angles, embrace flexibility, and find creative solutions. Embrace the spirit of innovation and adaptability in your thinking process.

3. Intuition and Introspection: Trust your instincts and tap into your intuition. Women often rely on their gut feelings to guide decision-making. Take time for introspection, reflect on your experiences, and trust your inner wisdom.

4. Resilience and Persistence: Women often demonstrate incredible resilience and perseverance in the face of challenges. Embrace setbacks as opportunities for growth, stay determined, and maintain a positive mindset even when the going gets tough.

Remember, thinking like a woman is not about excluding other perspectives or diminishing the value of male thinking. It's about recognizing and celebrating the unique strengths and perspectives that women offer. By embracing these qualities, you'll enhance your problem-solving abilities, foster inclusivity, and create a more dynamic and successful environment.

# Chapter 11 : Bridging the Gap: Note To Our Partners

Dear Partner,

As we approach the conclusion of this book, I want to take a moment to address you directly and express my deepest appreciation for embarking on this journey with me. Throughout these chapters, we have delved into the intricate details of understanding and decoding a man's mind from a woman's perspective. I want you to know I'm appreciative and this isn't just about just woman's perspective.

It's with deep appreciation and love that I want to emphasize the importance of your role as our partner. The goal of this book extends beyond simply sharing a woman's perspective. It seeks to celebrate and honor your opinions and feelings, recognizing their utmost significance in our relationship. By exploring the intricacies of understanding from both a man and a woman's standpoint, we aim to bridge the gap between couples, fostering a deeper sense of connection and unity.

This book serves as a testament to the value we place on your perspective, offering you the keys to unlock a profound understanding from a woman's point of view. It's essential to clarify that the purpose of this book is not to change who you're as an individual. Rather, it aims to equip you with invaluable tools and insights that will enhance the connection between us. Our desire is to feel understood, valued, and that our thoughts and emotions hold significance in our relationship.

If our journey together thus far has been riddled with incessant nagging, experiences of infidelity, or a lack of effective communication, isn't clear that there's room for growth and improvement. This realization prompts us to seek ways to strengthen our bond and become a more united couple. Understanding the female perspective is a key component in this journey.

Its important to note that decoding our minds does not require you to alter your fundamental self; rather, it offers you the opportunity to view things from our vantage point. By doing so, we can deepen our connection and nurture a thriving level of intimacy in our relationship. This is the end result that I want for all couples.

I invite you to explore various healthy approaches beyond the content shared in this book to foster growth and unity between us. Remember, our aim is not to divide efforts based on a 80/20 ratio. The 80/20 ratio in relationships refers to the idea that in a successful relationship, partner typically contributes 80% of the effort and the other partner contributes 20%. to become a unified force, sharing love, understanding, and mutual respect.

In addition to the insights presented throughout this chapter, communication, active listening, empathy, and openness play pivotal roles in strengthening our bond. Hearing and acknowledging each other's needs and concerns will enhance our understanding and create a foundation for a deeper connection.

As we progress on this incredible journey of growth and connection, please know that your efforts in understanding and decoding our perspective are sincerely cherished. Together, let us continue building a relationship that is rooted in love, respect, and a shared sense of purpose.

"I wholeheartedly invite you to continue your quest for self-growth and self-improvement. Education is a lifelong endeavor, and as we navigate this book together, I encourage you to make a conscious decision to embrace change. In the back of this book, you will find a mini journal specifically designed to aid you in this transformative process. I urge you to utilize this journal as a tool for reflection and self-discovery.

Take the time to jot down your thoughts, insights, and personal observations that arise as you delve deeper into the concepts shared. Treat it as a sacred space for fostering your personal growth and understanding. By engaging in this practice, you are not only investing in yourself but also demonstrating a true commitment to our relationship.

Your dedication to learning and evolving will further strengthen the bond we share. Embrace this opportunity to explore your own thoughts, emotions, and experiences, allowing them to shape and mold the person you are becoming. As we approach the final pages of this book, I want to express my sincere gratitude for your open-mindedness and willingness to embark on this transformative journey together.

Thank you for taking the time to absorb these words. I eagerly anticipate the road ahead, enriched by our commitment to growth and unity.

# CONCLUSION

It's important to note that "Thinking Like a Woman" does not mean generalizing or assuming that all women think and feel the same way. Every individual is unique, and experiences can vary greatly. The phrase is meant to encourage empathy, understanding, and an open-minded approach to bridging the gender gap and fostering healthier relationships. By adopting a mindset that seeks to understand women's perspectives can cultivate stronger connections, promote equality, and ultimately contribute to more fulfilling relationships.

Lastly-Understanding that women generally value thoughtfulness, attention to detail, and small gestures can go a long way. Showing appreciation and expressing affection regularly, whether through meaningful surprises, acts of service, or words of affirmation, can make a woman feel loved and valued.

However, it's important to approach these insights with flexibility and adaptability. Every individual is unique, and not all women may fit into these generalizations. Effective communication, mutual respect, and a genuine willingness to understand each other's needs are essential ingredients for a healthy and fulfilling relationship.

By thinking like a woman and decoding a man's mind from her perspective, individuals can foster understanding, empathy, and healthy relationships between genders. It's about acknowledging and appreciating the differences in how men may think, feel, and communicate, and creating an environment that values and respects those differences.

# THINK LIKE A WOMAN

## "Self-Discovery & Personal Growth"

IN ORDER TO THINK LIKE A WOMAN, YOU
MUST BE WILLING TO CHANGE WITHIN

by Coco Paye

# Important Notes From The Book

# THINGS I NEED TO CHANGE WITHIN

Writing down the things you need to change within yourself is important because it brings clarity, accountability, and serves as a personal growth tool. It helps you identify specific areas that require improvement, keeps you focused on your goals, and allows for regular reflection and tracking of progress towards change.

*Think Like A Woman*

# Thing's I Need To Change Within?

## THINGS I NEED FROM MY PARTNER

## THINGS I NEED TO CHANGE

## THINGS TO DO TO OVERCOME THOSE CHALLENGES

*Think Like A Woman*

# Positive Affirmation



*Think Like A Woman*

# Goal Tracker

When you make a subconscious decision to change, writing down your goals serves several important purposes:

1. Clarity: Writing down your goals brings clarity to your intentions. It forces you to articulate and define what you want to achieve, which helps in creating a clear vision for yourself.

2. Reinforcement: Writing down your goals helps reinforce your commitment to change. It serves as a constant reminder of what you want to accomplish and why it is important to you.

4. Focus: Having written goals provides a sense of direction and focus. It helps you prioritize your efforts and align your actions with your desired outcomes.

*Think Like A Woman*

# SETTING GOALS

## Goal 1:

**Specific** — What do I want to accomplish and why?

**Measurable** — How will I know when I have accomplished it?

**Achievable** — How can I accomplish this goal?

**Relevant** — Is this the right time for me to be working towards this goal?

**Timebound** — When do I want to accomplish this goal by?

## Goal 2:

**Specific.**

**Measurable.**

**Achievable.**

**Relevant.**

**Timebound.**

## Goal 3:

**Specific.**

**Measurable.**

**Achievable.**

**Relevant.**

**Timebound.**

## Goal 4:

**Specific.**

**Measurable.**

**Achievable.**

**Relevant.**

**Timebound.**

Today offers a fresh start and an opportunity to make positive changes, learn from past experiences, and move forward. Dwelling on the past can hinder your personal growth

MONDAY

TUESDAY

WEDNESDAY

THURSDAY

FRIDAY

SATURDAY

TO DO LIST

SUNDAY

NOTES

KEEP GOING!

# WEEKLY PLANNER

## MONDAY

## TUESDAY

## WEDNESDAY

## THURSDAY

## FRIDAY

## SATURDAY

## TO DO LIST

- ○
- ○
- ○
- ○
- ○
- ○
- ○

## SUNDAY

## NOTES

KEEP GOING!

# Daily Journal

# Daily Journal

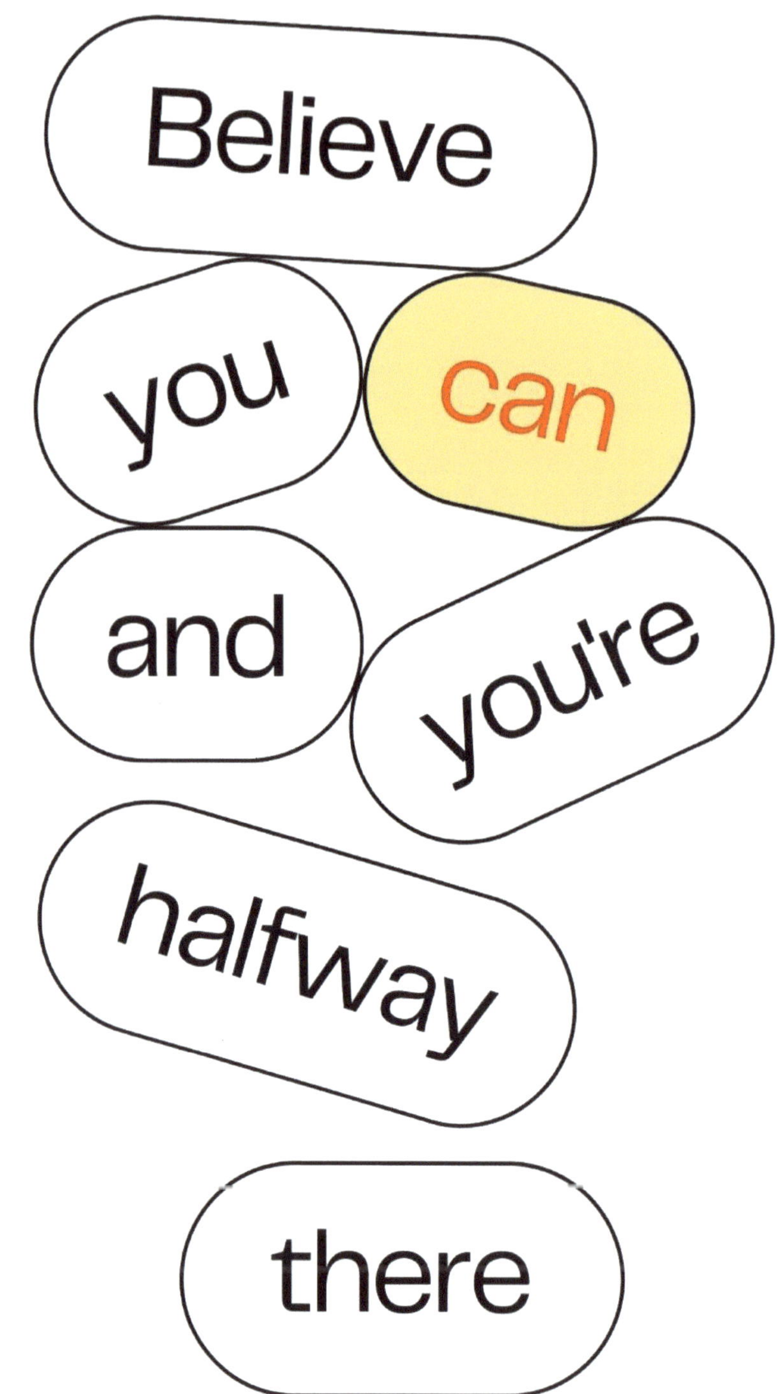
Believe
you
can
and
you're
halfway
there

www.ingramcontent.com/pod-product-compliance
Lightning Source LLC
Chambersburg PA
CBHW040921110726
48006CB00001B/21